CONTENTS

INTRODUCTION

Embarking on the exhilarating path of entrepreneurship is akin to embarking on a grand adventure. It grants you the freedom to pursue your lifelong passions, explore untapped creative possibilities, or formalize a thriving business venture. However, with this newfound excitement comes a myriad of new responsibilities and decisions that can often feel overwhelming.

Within the realm of entrepreneurship, one crucial decision stands above all others: selecting the ideal business structure that will propel your vision forward. It transcends a mere label; it requires a deep understanding of legal and tax regulations, effective collaboration with partners and associates, and the ability to make consensus-driven decisions, all while remaining mindful of your budgetary constraints. Additionally, safeguarding yourself from personal liability for corporate debts or claims becomes paramount, making the choice to establish a Limited Liability Company (LLC) all the more vital.

Whether you are starting from scratch or seeking to transform an existing partnership, this book offers a unique and refreshing perspective that will captivate and inspire readers. It is a gateway to fresh insights, innovative ideas, and captivating strategies that will empower you on your entrepreneurial journey.

The selection of a business structure profoundly influences every facet of your venture, from day-to-day operations to tax obligations and the level of personal asset protection. Among the array of business structures available, Limited Liability Companies (LLCs) have emerged as the preferred choice for countless entrepreneurs, thanks to their attractive blend of tax advantages and liability protections.

An LLC is not just an ordinary business entity; it represents a dynamic fusion of corporate elements and partnership dynamics, custom-tailored to offer unparalleled benefits for business owners.

By delving into the intricacies of limited liability companies, you will gain profound insights into how they can serve as the ideal foundation for your entrepreneurial aspirations.

It's important to note that while LLCs share similarities across jurisdictions, each state may have specific laws governing their formation and operation. Furthermore, certain industries, such as banking and insurance, may impose restrictions on forming an LLC.

Limited liability organizations provide invaluable forms of protection for business owners. At the forefront of these safeguards is the limitation of personal liabilities. An LLC ensures that the company's debts remain separate from the personal assets of its owners.

Moreover, owners enjoy protection from the actions of other owners, employees, or even themselves, in matters pertaining to the LLC. Additionally, an LLC shields itself from liability for any personal obligations arising from the conduct of its staff employees. Collectively, these safeguards create a secure and robust financial environment for the company and its members.

While establishing an LLC may not be an insurmountable task, it is crucial to navigate the proper procedures to ensure a solid foundation for both the present and the future. This comprehensive guide transcends the ordinary, offering you a transformative and unparalleled understanding of the subject matter. Within these pages, you will embark on a captivating journey, exploring every facet of forming and managing an LLC.

Prepare to be enthralled by an abundance of fresh perspectives, novel strategies, and cutting-edge insights.

Each chapter unravels a new dimension, equipping you with the knowledge to make informed decisions and chart your entrepreneurial voyage towards unprecedented growth and prosperity. From legal intricacies to strategic planning and beyond, this book serves as your compass, guiding you through the labyrinth of entrepreneurship with confidence and clarity.

Are you ready to pioneer your own unique path to entrepreneurial success and fulfillment? The time has come to seize the reins and embark on this transformative expedition.

Within these pages, the extraordinary awaits, beckoning you to unlock your full potential and embrace a future filled with unlimited possibilities. Your entrepreneurial journey begins now.

CHAPTER 1: A CONCISE REVIEW OF LIMITED LIABILITY COMPANY (LLC)

What exactly is a Limited Liability Company (LLC)?

The concept of an LLC was first acknowledged by the Internal Revenue Service (IRS) in 1980, after Wyoming and Florida made legislative strides to establish the LLC format in the 1970s. Today, every state offers this business structure, which blends the features of a corporation, partnership, and sole proprietorship into a single entity.

LLCs offer members, who are equivalent to the owners of the company, protection from personal liability much like a corporation. However, they avoid the sting of double taxation by adopting a pass-through tax system akin to a partnership or sole proprietorship.

This hybrid entity offers entrepreneurs the independence to manage their businesses without the regulatory complexities of a corporation while still safeguarding their personal assets from business liabilities.

Despite their pass-through tax benefits, partnerships and sole proprietorships don't provide their owners with limited liability.

In contrast, corporations do offer limited liability but face double taxation. To avoid double taxation, corporations can elect S Corporation status, yet they still don't enjoy the tax advantages of an LLC.

Members of an LLC can self-manage or appoint a manager for the job. The LLC's management can be manager-managed or member-managed, as per the members' discretion. To form an LLC, the owner must file Articles of Organization with the Secretary of State.

The LLC's operational agreement dictates the guidelines for its governance, such as:

> Identifying whether the LLC is managed by its members.
> Outlining members' rights and benefits.
> Describing each member's ownership share.
> Detailing the allocation of profits and losses.
> Laying down the protocols for ownership transfer.

In the absence of an LLC charter or specific provisions in the document, state regulations apply.

Wyoming was the pioneer in legalizing LLCs in 1977, driven by the Hamilton Bros Oil company's bid to replicate its advantageous liability and tax structure in Panama. However, the ambiguous interpretation of the Kintner rules by the IRS and the courts delayed other states' acceptance of the LLC format. It wasn't until 1988, when the IRS ruled that LLCs were taxable as partnerships, that other states started adopting their own LLC statutes. By 1996, all 50 states had LLC legislation. The next year, the IRS implemented the "check the box" (CTB) entity classification, thereby rendering the Kintner rules obsolete.

LLCs are state-regulated, owned by members, and require state registration. They offer a combination of simplicity, flexibility, and protection, making them a favored choice among entrepreneurs. LLCs are open to various types of owners, including individuals, businesses, and foreign entities. Banks and insurers, however, are not eligible to form LLCs.

LLCs have a default tax status as pass-through entities, but they can choose to be taxed like corporations. However, if an LLC engages in fraudulent activities or breaches legal and reporting norms, members can be sued by creditors. The members of an LLC have the freedom to devise a flexible management structure as per their operating agreement, as long as it complies with state law. State statutes often provide default rules for LLC governance.

As of August 1, 2013, Delaware law has imposed fiduciary duties of care and loyalty on the managers and managing members of a Delaware LLC. Parties to an LLC can modify or waive fiduciary duties in their LLC agreements, with the exception of the implied covenant of good faith and fair dealing.

LLCs must register in all states where they conduct business. Defining "conducting business" can be complex, as each state has its own criteria and laws. Merely forming an LLC in any state may not fulfill legal requirements. An LLC formed in one state may be required to register as a foreign LLC in other states if its owner(s), employees, or base of operations are located in those states.

The steps to form an LLC include selecting a unique company name, filing the articles of organization, creating an operating agreement, obtaining necessary licenses and permits, and, in some states, publishing an announcement about your LLC formation.
One crucial difference between an LLC and a partnership is that an LLC shields its owners' personal assets from business liabilities.

Both LLCs and partnerships allow income to flow through to the owners, who are responsible for the associated taxes.

In the absence of a business continuation agreement, the departure or death of an owner may necessitate the dissolution and reformation of the LLC.

CHAPTER 2: THE INTRIGUING MERITS OF ESTABLISHING AN LLC FOR SMALL ENTERPRISES

The Positives of an LLC are Unmistakable

The rationale for establishing an LLC is supported by a plethora of compelling arguments. Even a single benefit would be enough to persuade a sole proprietor to transition. Let's delve into these merits with more depth.

Streamlined Creation of an LLC
Forming an LLC can be an uncomplicated and swift endeavor. In a matter of a few hours, you can fill out and dispatch all the needed paperwork with a nominal fee.

Onerous paperwork like operating agreements, minutes of meetings, company archives, resolutions, and annual reports are not prerequisites. Moreover, the flexibility to form an LLC at your own site exists, and the number of members required is fewer than for corporations. LLCs bring a refreshing simplicity to corporate operations.

While establishing an LLC brings some routine responsibilities and filings, usually annual, it's important to note the overall cost and paperwork is minimal. Keep in mind the fees to set up an LLC may vary across states – for instance, it's a meager $50 in Colorado while it is $520 in Massachusetts. Yet, the cost of annual reporting for your LLC, which may range from $0 to $520 depending on your state, can usually be offset by your LLC's tax savings.

Liability Reduction
An LLC offers a protective veil between your personal and business assets. If a lawsuit is launched against your LLC, it's your company, not you, that is in the line of fire.

While a business's assets might be seized, your personal possessions like home, car, or investments generally remain untouched. Conversely, in sole proprietorships or partnerships, a lawsuit against your entity or you personally could result in the claimant going after your personal belongings to settle the debt.
However, establishing an LLC doesn't render you invincible to all liabilities. For example, if you personally guarantee a business loan, you will be personally liable regardless of your business's legal structure.

Choose Your Tax Status
The formation of an LLC opens up a buffet of tax options. Single-member LLCs and multi-member

LLCs are typically taxed as sole proprietorships and partnerships respectively, using pass-through taxation.

This means your business earnings are filed along with your personal tax return, bypassing the double taxation applicable to corporations. Yet, you still have the option to tax your LLC as a C-corp or S-corp, providing potential tax savings and business deductions.

The Freedom of Management

LLCs allow either a hired manager or the owners (members) to run the day-to-day operations. This versatility empowers you to manage your business in a way that best suits your needs, a flexibility that corporations typically do not enjoy. If at any point you wish to delegate management duties to someone else, it can be done without board approval.

Elevate Your Credibility

Trust is a vital currency in business, and forming an LLC can give you an edge. Setting up an LLC reflects your commitment to your enterprise and your willingness to take the necessary steps to legitimize it. The requirement to incorporate "LLC" in your business name can serve as a powerful signifier of your credibility.

Profit Sharing Modularity

LLCs allow members the flexibility to decide how profits are distributed, which need not correlate to their ownership percentage. This could be especially useful when a member agrees to dedicate more time and energy to the business, and members mutually agree to a profit distribution that doesn't mirror their ownership stakes. However, there are some restrictions, like when the LLC's solvency is at stake or when liabilities outweigh assets.

Potential to Secure Business Loans

Securing financing is a likely eventuality for your business. Often, small business loans are more economical than giving away equity. While getting a loan may be challenging, forming an LLC can improve your odds of securing one. It lends a layer of credibility and assurance to lenders that the borrower is serious about fulfilling their repayment obligations.

Protect Your Brand

Forming an LLC reserves your business name within your state, preventing any other company from using a similar name. It's a straightforward and effective way to safeguard your brand. However, it doesn't prevent others in different states from using the same name, necessitating a trademark for comprehensive protection.

Open a Solo 401(k)

If you don't have any employees, being an LLC allows you to open a solo 401(k), often referred to as a self-employed 401(k).

Functioning much like traditional 401(k)s, these plans enable you to make pretax contributions to your retirement savings account, which can be invested in a variety of ways. The contribution limits are typically higher than regular 401(k)s, allowing for even greater retirement savings.

CHAPTER 3: EVALUATING THE BENEFITS OF AN LLC FOR YOUR ENTERPRISE

The structure of your business not only influences your personal liability, but also affects your potential for capital procurement, tax duties, and the tax amount you're obliged to pay. Before making your company an official entity within your state, the decision about the type of business structure to choose is a pivotal one. Aside from deciding on the business form, many businesses need to secure essential licenses, permissions, and a tax ID number.

Choose thoughtfully, as while it is possible to transition to a different business form later, restrictions may arise due to geographical limitations. Such changes can trigger potential problems like unforeseen dissolution and tax complications.

LLCs (Limited Liability Companies) often prove to be a worthwhile choice for businesses with moderate to high risk, entrepreneurs aiming to safeguard their major personal assets, and business owners who prefer a lower tax rate than what a corporation would impose. An LLC provides a blend of advantages from both business and partnership structures.

Typically, an LLC grants protection from personal liability; in the event your LLC declares bankruptcy, your personal belongings, like your car, house, and savings accounts, are not put at risk. Profits and losses can be transferred to your personal income, avoiding corporation taxes. However, keep in mind that LLC members are considered self-employed and must contribute self-employment tax payments towards Social Security and Medicare.

Additionally, the lifespan of an LLC may be limited in certain states. When a member leaves or joins, some states might require the LLC to disband and re-establish with new members, unless a pre-existing written agreement for share transfer is in place.

Who is a prime candidate for forming an LLC? Essentially, anyone who is starting a business, or already runs one as a sole proprietor or as part of a partnership, qualifies. Although nearly any kind of business can be run under an LLC (often used to own rental or commercial properties), some states stipulate that business owners establish a particular form of LLC known as a Professional Limited Liability Company (PLLC).

LLCs offer tangible benefits to small businesses. Key advantages include:
>Asset Protection: The "limited liability" part of an LLC implies personal protection. As a small business owner, an LLC serves as your safety net, reducing personal liability. In the case of company-related lawsuits, liens, or debts, only the assets of the company (not your

personal assets) are at stake.

Pass-Through Taxation: LLCs grant pass-through tax benefits to small business owners, which means company profits are reported on personal income tax returns and subjected to personal tax rates. LLC owners may also qualify for a pass-through tax deduction under the Tax Cut and Jobs Act, which may allow them to deduct up to 20% of their annual net business income.

Flexibility & Ease of Operation: An LLC is one of the simplest business entities to establish and operate, offering significant flexibility. There is no cap on the number of owners a company can have, and they allow the option to appoint specific managers.

Credibility: Forming an LLC helps build trust with your customers and enhances your business legitimacy.

Before deciding to form an LLC, small business owners should weigh factors such as the degree of risk, potential revenue, public trust, and the need for liability protection. It's important to separate any business that carries risk from its owner legally, a concept known as limited liability protection. This protection ensures the owner's personal assets are secure if the company is sued or incurs debt.

The flexible tax options offered by an LLC can be advantageous for a small business that generates a steady profit. LLC owners can opt for either the corporation's (S Corp) tax classification or pass-through taxation. Corporations and LLCs both provide limited liability protection, but the best choice for your business depends on its specific needs.

Forming a corporation might be beneficial for a business that heavily relies on external investors due to the taxation method. However, for any small business not requiring outside investors, an LLC would be a more tax-efficient choice.

Credibility is also a key factor in choosing the type of business. Simply establishing an LLC can confer a degree of credibility and trust with customers, which is vital for any business.

CHAPTER 4: CREATING A LIMITED LIABILITY COMPANY (LLC)

Step 1: Select a Name for Your LLC
Deciding on a suitable name for your LLC is the initial step. Your LLC's name must be unique and not conflict with other companies already registered in the state.

It should also contain the term "Limited Liability Company," or its abbreviation (LLC or L.L.C.). Certain words, like 'Bank,' 'Trust,' or 'Insurance,' might require additional paperwork or licensed individuals to be part of the LLC.

Step 2: Choose a Registered Agent
A registered agent is an individual or business entity authorized to receive and send legal papers on behalf of your LLC. It can be an LLC member or a professional service. The agent must have a physical street address in the state and be available during regular business hours.

Step 3: File the Articles of Organization
After choosing a name and a registered agent, you need to file the Articles of Organization with your state's LLC filing office, usually the Secretary of State's office. The Articles of Organization, a straightforward document, is primarily used to record the LLC's name, its purpose, the name and address of the registered agent, and the members' information. Filing fees for the Articles of Organization vary across different states.

Additionally, a registered agent is required to be available for receiving legal documents, often known as service of process. This includes formal notifications of legal actions filed against an LLC, which consist of orders and complaints, also known as "Notices of Litigation." The agent also collects other court papers such as subpoenas and garnishment orders.

Step 4: Create an LLC Operating Agreement
Most states mandate that an LLC should have an operating agreement. It is also strongly recommended that this agreement be in writing, though oral agreements are permitted in many states. The operating agreement is a contract outlining how the LLC will be managed by its members. Even if you're a single-member LLC, an operational agreement is critical, as it establishes your recognition of the LLC's separate existence, which can help prevent the piercing of the corporate veil.

Step 5: Register your LLC with the state
To legally establish your LLC, you must file a Certificate of Organization, Certificate of Formation, or Articles of Organization with the Secretary of State's office or another department that handles business filings in the state where your LLC is being formed.

After forming the LLC, an employment identification number (EIN) application must be filed with the IRS. This number will be used by your LLC to identify itself on all bank accounts and tax returns.

Step 7: Set up a Business Bank Account
Setting up a business bank account is a best practice that should be adopted by anyone establishing an LLC.

Keeping personal and business finances separate is critical and is a primary factor considered by courts when deciding whether to pierce the LLC's corporate veil.

Step 8: Register your business in other states, if required
If your LLC intends to operate in other states besides the one in which it was formed, you must register or "foreign qualify" in each of those states.

This usually involves applying for authorization with the Secretary of State and maintaining a registered agent.
In conclusion, while establishing an LLC may seem daunting, breaking down the process into these detailed steps can help navigate the complexities and requirements, making it a manageable task.

CHAPTER 5: NAVIGATING THE MAZE: SIDESTEPPING PITFALLS AND ERRORS WHEN LAUNCHING AN LLC

Enthusiasm and focus on the end goal of forming an LLC are crucial when navigating the business landscape. The enhanced professional image and the trust it cultivates among potential clients make the journey worthwhile.

However, tunnel vision can cause you to overlook the subtle but critical details that can impact your business dramatically. This chapter will unveil the traps and missteps that entrepreneurs often miss during their journey of launching an LLC.

Navigating Common Missteps When Establishing an LLC
Oversight in Declaring a Business Structure: When you bag your first client, it's easy to dive headfirst into operations, focusing on expanding your client base and revenue streams. However, this enthusiasm might cause you to overlook the fundamental step of declaring your business structure. The chosen business entity can influence your taxation and susceptibility to specific risks. By ignoring this step, you unintentionally expose your business to unnecessary liabilities. The process of defining your business begins with entity registration – a crucial step towards establishing a secure foundation for your business.

Misjudgment in Opting for an LLC: Selecting the right business structure is crucial. Entrepreneurs often falter, gravitating towards forming an LLC when another structure might serve their needs better.

The variance lies in factors such as tax filing methods, the desired distinction between personal and business assets, and control over your business. For instance, an advertising professional may register their business as an LLC in its first year, only to find out during tax season that they might have reaped more benefits by operating as a sole proprietorship. We recommend consulting a tax expert or attorney to guide you in this decision-making process.

Incorrect LLC Type Declaration: Registering your LLC correctly is just as important as deciding to form one. The tax implications imposed by the IRS heavily depend on your LLC registration type. For instance, you need to decide if your LLC is "manager-managed" (run by the owner) or "member-managed" (governed by a group of individuals). Additionally, your LLC can be "at-will" or "term", outlining the fate of your company's assets in case of shutdown.

Consult a tax professional or legal counsel to discern the most suitable choice.

Failure in Maintaining Your LLC: There's a common misconception that an LLC, once established, functions indefinitely like stock shares. However, an LLC is an organization, not a document, and requires regular updating and maintenance.

Failing to keep your LLC current can potentially expose your firm to liabilities. In essence, owning an LLC is akin to maintaining a car – it requires constant care beyond annual payments, including ongoing compliance and recordkeeping.

Overlooking Compliance Maintenance: The process of forming an LLC doesn't end with filing the initial paperwork. Post formation, you need to ensure your LLC is compliant.

Failure to do so can risk piercing the corporate veil, endangering your personal assets. Stay compliant by keeping your business name on all corporate documents, submitting yearly reports, keeping personal and business finances separate, and consulting a legal expert to understand your state's requirements.

Lack of Proper Business License: In their pursuit of forming an LLC, some business owners forget to ascertain if they need a business license. While both LLC and business license build trust among your clients, they serve different purposes.

The necessity of a business license is dependent on state-specific rules and regulations as well as your occupation. Don't overlook local requirements; even if your state doesn't mandate it, your town or county might require a permit.

Reliance on Online Legal Documents: The internet is a trove of information with countless forms and templates.

While they can save time and money, indiscriminate use of these documents can lead to trouble. Always ensure you thoroughly vet these templates before integrating them into your LLC. Consulting a legal expert can provide clarity on ambiguous terms and ensure the paperwork is robust.

Setting up LLC in the Wrong State: It's imperative to ascertain the correct state for establishing your LLC. Some entrepreneurs opt to register their LLC in different states for perceived tax benefits. However, the decision should be based on the specifics of your business and location. While an out-of-state LLC may offer tax benefits, remember that you'll need a registered agent in the state where the LLC is formed.

Not Seeking Proper Legal Advice: It's not wrong to file LLC paperwork on your own, particularly if you're a single-member LLC with simple circumstances.

However, for complex situations such as conducting business across multiple jurisdictions, partnering with someone, or contemplating an S-Corp, legal advice can be beneficial. The upfront cost of legal counsel is a deductible business expense that could potentially save you money in the long run.

Misbelief of Invincibility: Forming an LLC is indeed a significant milestone, but don't fall into the trap of believing it makes you impervious to risks. Even if your LLC is acquitted in a lawsuit, legal fees could still be a financial burden. Remember, an LLC aids in separating personal and business assets but cannot fully insulate you from risk.

The Most Grave Error – Absence of LLC Insurance: Forming an LLC typically provides a shield between your personal and business assets. However, your business assets like expensive equipment or software subscriptions are not protected from lawsuits. Even if you're at the early stages of your business, having LLC insurance is crucial. Just one lawsuit can jeopardize your business's future. Avoiding these pitfalls and seeking expert advice can put you on the path to establishing a successful LLC.

CHAPTER 6: TRANSITIONING YOUR EXISTING VENTURE TO AN LLC

Are you considering upgrading your current business structure to a Limited Liability Company (LLC)? It's vital to comprehend the array of businesses that can metamorphose into LLCs, the necessary requirements, and the likely legal and tax implications before embarking on this endeavor.

Understanding the Uniform Act on Limited Liability Companies
To pave the way for LLCs, each state in the U.S. has adopted the Uniform Private Company Act or an equivalent variant. These acts enable the creation of an LLC for any lawful business operation, making an LLC an ideal entity for nearly any business type due to its immense adaptability. The formation of an LLC demands filing articles of organization with the respective state.

LLCs boast two primary advantages: they offer liability protection akin to a corporation and their 'pass-through' status means LLC owners evade the double taxation often experienced by corporation shareholders.

Business Structures Eligible for LLC Conversion
An LLC is owned by its members, who can be individuals, partnerships, corporations, or even other LLCs. Any entity legally authorized to form and join an LLC can alter its status to a limited liability company. This includes:

        Solo businesses.
        Corporations.
        Multiple LLCs.

However, certain business entities like banks and insurance companies are legally prohibited from becoming an LLC, and a few states cap the number of legal entities that can merge into an LLC.

Navigating the Conversion Process
The transformation to an LLC varies based on the existing business structure. A sole proprietorship, for instance, needs to file its articles of incorporation with the state business registration office. For a corporation, shareholders must unanimously agree to the conversion, signifying that the corporation's assets and liabilities are transferred to the new LLC. In the case of a partnership, all partners must consent to the change.

Notably, shifting to an LLC can reduce tax burdens by allowing business owners to deduct business taxes from their personal income. This is a considerable advantage considering that most small-business owners (86.6%) operate under the sole proprietorship structure.

Sole Proprietorship vs. LLC

Before proceeding with the conversion, understanding the differences between a sole proprietorship and an LLC is crucial. While the former is an entity owned by a single individual, the latter can have multiple members. An LLC distinguishes the business from the owners, providing limited liability, whereas in a sole proprietorship, you shoulder all financial obligations.

Deciding to transition from a sole proprietorship to an LLC requires careful thought. Key benefits of operating an LLC include reduced liability, pass-through taxation, and relative ease of setup. However, bear in mind that an LLC might also necessitate additional tax forms and prevent the issuance of stock.

Transitioning from a Sole Proprietorship to an LLC

The conversion process depends on your state's regulations. Generally, the steps include revoking the "Doing Business As" (DBA) name of your sole proprietorship, choosing a registered agent, submitting articles of organization, creating an operating agreement, and applying for an Employer Identification Number (EIN).

The distinction between personal and business assets is key to maintaining limited liability. Shifting from a sole proprietorship to an LLC can safeguard your personal assets, but it might increase your tax and fee obligations. Therefore, it's recommended to seek professional legal advice to navigate this complex decision.

Conversion Possibilities Across States

The possibility of converting from an LLC to a corporation, or vice versa, is available in many states including Alabama, Arkansas, California, Colorado, Delaware, Florida, Georgia, Hawaii, Iowa, Idaho, Indiana, Kansas, Louisiana, Massachusetts, Maine, Michigan, Minnesota, Nevada, Ohio, Oklahoma, Oregon, Rhode Island, South Carolina, South Dakota, Tennessee, Texas, Utah, Virginia, Washington, Wisconsin, and Wyoming.

Only in Alaska, Kentucky, and West Virginia can a corporation convert into an LLC. On the other hand, Arizona, Connecticut, the District of Columbia, Illinois, Maryland, Missouri, Mississippi, Montana, Nebraska, New Hampshire, New Jersey, New York, Pennsylvania, and Vermont prohibit such conversions.

CHAPTER 7: BUILDING THE FINANCIAL FOUNDATION FOR YOUR LLC

As a budding LLC owner, mastering the art of accounting is a fundamental part of your entrepreneurial journey. LLCs offer an advantageous tax structure for its members while eliminating the rigidity often encountered in corporate management, making it a favorable choice for many entrepreneurs.

Setting up an LLC

Crucial aspects of managing an LLC encompass the triumvirate of sales, marketing, and most importantly, accounting. It's accounting that fortifies the limited liability shield, which secures your personal assets against the debts and liabilities incurred by the business.

LLCs, unlike corporations, come with a lighter administrative burden when it comes to record-keeping requirements. However, some states may mandate the filing of an annual report. Since LLCs operate as pass-through entities by default, income and losses get reported on each member's individual tax returns. Additionally, a considerable number of LLC members also owe self-employment tax. It's crucial to consult a tax professional for an understanding of how state and federal taxes apply to your LLC.

The Heart of LLC Accounting

The heart of an LLC's accounting system is much akin to that of a conventional corporation. It involves maintaining a general ledger and a chart of accounts, capturing all financial transactions. Typical transactions that an LLC would record include billing a client, receiving payment, recording a supplier's invoice, paying a vendor, tracking fixed assets, disbursing wages, recognizing asset depreciation, and recording loan transactions.

The General Ledger: The Backbone of LLC Accounting

The general ledger serves as the backbone of any LLC's accounting framework, akin to most business structures. Think of it as a business diary that captures the ins and outs of all financial transactions. It chronicles details of various business facets such as cash flows, investments, property, major equipment, and also the liabilities like loans, credit card balances, and other payables.

Decisions on Tax Structure

Before laying the groundwork for a robust accounting system, you must select a tax structure for your LLC. When you register your LLC, decide whether you want it to be taxed as a corporation, partnership, or sole proprietorship. Remember to choose the entity type that best suits your tax circumstances, not necessarily the legal structure of your LLC.

Setting up the Accounting System

Kick-starting the accounting process involves creating a chart of accounts that represent all your business's income, expenses, assets, liabilities, and equity divisions. Document every transaction, whether it's cash received, checks issued, equity withdrawals, or equity infusions.

Choosing an Accounting Method

When it comes to initiating an LLC's accounting system, you have the option to choose between accrual-based accounting or cash-based accounting. The accrual method recognizes income when it's earned and expenses when they're incurred, while the cash method records income upon receipt of cash and expenses only after the bills are paid.

The accrual method, while demanding more complex accounting, produces more accurate financial statements. Conversely, the cash method is less accurate but is simpler to use, making it a favorite among small businesses with limited accounting resources.

Each method has its advantages and drawbacks. The cash method's simplicity appeals to small businesses, while the accrual method offers a more accurate representation of your company's monthly income and expenses. Remember, the choice of accounting method can significantly impact when you pay taxes, so choose wisely.

Each step taken in setting up your LLC's accounting system builds a sturdy financial foundation that will serve you well as your business grows. Ensure you familiarize yourself with the different aspects of LLC accounting to navigate this journey smoothly. With each mastered concept, you are one step closer to building a thriving LLC.

CHAPTER 8: MASTERING YOUR BUSINESS'S FINANCIAL HEALTH

Consider this comprehensive guide your ally in the battle of small business finance management. By diving into key financial jargon, exploring the nuances of maintaining a clean credit score, understanding the process of securing a business loan, and more, we aim to equip you with the tools necessary to confidently manage your organization's financial landscape.

Keeping Personal and Business Finances Apart

As a business owner, the first and arguably most important rule is maintaining clear lines between personal and business finances. This practice is imperative not only for organization and taxation purposes, but also for your legal protection. By clearly separating your personal and business finances, you not only streamline your bookkeeping processes and business tax requirements, but you also safeguard your personal assets against potential legal hurdles that your business may encounter.

Choosing the Ideal Business Bank Account

One of the simplest ways to segregate personal and business finances is by opening a dedicated business bank account.

The key to managing your firm's financials effectively lies in choosing the right bank account, which requires thoughtful consideration of numerous factors, including comparisons between savings and checking accounts, ways to avoid monthly service fees, transaction limits, wire transfer exemptions, cash deposit restrictions, ATM usage, and the availability of online and mobile banking services. Your ultimate goal should be to find a bank that not only securely houses your funds but also aids in the daily financial management of your enterprise.

Decoding the Basics of Business Accounting

Once you have your business bank account up and running, it's time to familiarize yourself with the fundamental principles of small business accounting. Grasping basic accounting terminology and understanding essential documents might seem daunting, especially if you're new to the field. However, these concepts will enable you to comprehend how accounting impacts your business's finances and equip you to select appropriate accounting software or hire a skilled professional if needed.

Delving Into Essential Accounting Vocabulary

As you navigate the financial management terrain of your startup, you'll encounter several recurring terms. Knowing these terms will make other financial management practices less daunting. Here are a few key terms you should become familiar with:

Gross Profit: This is your total sales revenue, minus any costs of goods sold or other charges.

Expenses: These are costs incurred in the course of running your business, such as rent, salaries, taxes, and more.

Net Income: This is what remains after deducting all expenses from your gross profit.

Cash Flow: This is the difference between the cash at the start and the end of an accounting period, which includes money coming in and going out.

Breakeven Point: This is the point at which your total revenues and total expenses are equal.

Managing Important Business Accounting Documents

Operating a small business involves a lot of paperwork, especially when it comes to finance. Proper financial documentation is essential for tax filing, loan applications, and internal revenue and expense tracking.

The four key accounting documents you should regularly maintain are:

Balance Sheet: This snapshot of your company's financial health at any given time lists your assets, liabilities, and equity.

Income Statement: Also known as the profit and loss statement, this document highlights your annual revenues and expenses.

Cash Flow Statement: This tracks your business's cash flow over a given period.

Revenue Forecast: This is an estimate of your future earnings, helping you determine budgetary allowances and expected profits.

Leveraging Accounting Software

Manual accounting can be overwhelming, which is where accounting software comes in. These tools can automate and simplify your bookkeeping tasks, saving you significant time and effort. They keep your essential accounting documents a few clicks away and can generate these documents automatically.

Understanding Business Taxes

After separating personal and business finances and organizing your books, you need to understand and comply with tax laws.

Non-compliance can result in penalties, business loss, and even criminal charges. Taxes can often be a complex part of small business finance, but it's crucial to understand them to avoid potential issues.

Mastering Credit Scores

Controlling your credit scores is vital for your business's financial health. At some point, you'll need access to credit, whether for leasing property or equipment, getting a business credit card, or securing a small business loan. Your personal and business credit histories will greatly influence your financing options.

Exploring Financing and Loan Options

Once you have a handle on the above processes, you may want to explore additional financing for your business. Understanding the variety of loans available and their qualification criteria will help you better plan your business's finances.

You might also consider some innovative financing options like peer-to-peer (P2P) lending sites, which connect entrepreneurs to private and institutional investors, initial coin offerings (ICOs), which leverage public ledgers and blockchain systems, government-sponsored loans, or even reaching out to your personal network. It's all about finding the right solution for your unique business needs.

CHAPTER 9: UNTANGLING THE TAX IMPLICATIONS FOR AN LLC

The fiscal architecture of a Limited Liability Company (LLC) closely mimics that of a "pass-through" model, aligning it with the structures of a partnership or sole proprietorship.

This translates to the fiscal wins and setbacks of the company being directly experienced by the owners (or 'members') on their personal tax submissions. Notwithstanding the fact that a few states might levy an annual LLC tax, the federal income tax typically doesn't apply to the LLC itself.
So, how do we unravel LLC tax calculations?

The IRS views your LLC through the lens of a partnership or a sole proprietorship, contingent on the number of members in your organization.

Solo-Owned LLCs:
In instances where the LLC has a single member, the IRS regards them akin to self-employed entities when it comes to taxation. The implication here is that such LLCs aren't accountable for paying taxes and don't need to file a tax return with the IRS. As the lone owner, you're required to report all the financial highs and lows of the LLC on your personal 1040 tax return.

Depending upon the nature and specifics of your business, you may need to attach additional schedules with your 1040. These could include Schedule C for reporting business income, Schedule SE for self-employment tax or Schedule E for declaring income from rental properties and investments. If you choose to retain profits in the company account at the fiscal year-end for future expenses or business expansion, taxes must be paid on these earnings.
Multiple-Member LLCs:
In cases where LLCs have multiple owners, the IRS categorizes them similar to partnerships for taxation purposes. Like single-owner LLCs, multi-member LLCs also don't pay taxes on business income. Instead, each member of the LLC is required to report taxes on their personal federal tax returns (accompanied by a Schedule E) on their portion of the profits. The LLC's operating agreement should specify each member's distributive share, i.e., their percentage of profits and losses. This distributive share is subject to taxation.

Irrespective of how the distributive shares are divided among members, the IRS assumes each member receives their full share of the distribution annually. This means that even if the LLC does not distribute all (or any) of the funds to the members, each member is still obliged to pay tax on their entire distributive share. This taxation model can have significant implications, especially when the LLC members decide to reinvest profits back into the business for expansion or inventory purchase. Despite these profits not being distributed, each member is still liable to pay tax on their portion of these retained earnings.

Opting for a Corporate Tax Structure:
If your LLC frequently retains a substantial portion of its earnings, you may want to consider electing a corporate tax structure.

By submitting IRS Form Caucasian Entity Taxonomy Election and choosing the corporate tax classification, LLCs can opt to be taxed as a corporation. A flat tax rate of 21% is applied to all regular "C" corporations' earnings. Compared to the top three personal income tax brackets, which range from 32% to 37% and apply to high-earning LLC members, this flat rate can significantly reduce the tax liability.
However, there's a double taxation caveat when it comes to distributing earnings from a C corporation to its owners. Firstly, the corporation needs to pay the 21% tax rate, and subsequently, the members must pay personal income taxes on the received dividends at capital gain rates, which can go up to 23.8%.

Therefore, the potential savings from opting for the corporate tax structure might not be as substantial as they appear at first glance. Retained earnings, on the other hand, are only subject to the 21% corporate tax rate, making this an attractive option for businesses that plan to reinvest a substantial part of their earnings back into the business.

State Taxes for LLCs:
In many states, LLC members are required to pay state taxes on their earnings in a similar fashion to federal taxes, meaning that the members pay taxes on their personal returns rather than the LLC paying as an entity. However, in some states, the LLC itself may also be subject to an additional tax based on the company's income.

CHAPTER 10: SAFEGUARDING YOUR PERSONAL ASSETS WITH AN LLC

An LLC or a "Limited Liability Company" is a type of business organization that offers a protective shield for its owners, shielding them from liability.

These protections are fortified by the laws of the state where the LLC is registered. An LLC creates a distinct boundary between the business entity and its owners, known as "Members", ensuring that personal and business assets remain separate.

Limited liability safeguards the members of the LLC from the debts and liabilities of the company, essentially making sure that a member's personal assets such as homes or other private property cannot be seized by creditors to settle company debts. This effectively limits a member's financial risk to their investment in the company, making an LLC an ideal vehicle for small business owners looking to expand their ventures while maintaining a safety net for their personal assets.

Why Establish an LLC?
Entrepreneurs opt for an LLC to create a firewall between their private assets and the liabilities of their business. When managed correctly, the structure of an LLC can prove to be a formidable barrier for a business creditor attempting to seize a member's personal assets, which may include homes, vehicles, or other personal valuables.
LLCs are not just limited to running businesses.

They can also be used by individuals to hold passive assets or assets that generate income. Since an LLC is a distinct legal entity, it can own a variety of assets such as real estate, intellectual property, and trademarks.

Personal Accountability for Actions and Conduct of Members
The protection granted by an LLC extends to the misdeeds and unpaid debts of other members and employees. This means your personal assets are secure even if the company is found culpable for these actions, though the assets of the LLC itself might be at risk. However, the member who enacted the negligent or unlawful action can be personally liable.

For example, if an employee injures a pedestrian while performing a task for the LLC and is found to be at fault, the assets of the LLC and the responsible employee may be seized to settle a legal judgment. Your personal property, however, remains unaffected.
Liability for Your Own Actions
Any negligent or unlawful action you commit while managing your LLC can render you personally

liable. Such instances could include inflicting injury upon someone due to negligence, withholding taxes from employee earnings, committing fraudulent acts, or any other unlawful or negligent action that harms the LLC, an individual, or another business.

One of the most critical aspects here is the commingling of personal and company finances and activities. If a court establishes that personal and business finances were mixed, it may rule that the LLC is not a separate entity and all members are therefore personally accountable for the debts and obligations of the LLC.

To avoid this, ensure the following:

- Honestly disclose all relevant financial information to clients, creditors, and suppliers.
- Inject sufficient capital into the business to meet its financial obligations.
- Set up a separate business bank account for the LLC and secure a tax ID (EIN) from the IRS.
- Draft a comprehensive written operating agreement detailing the management and operation of the LLC.

Consider a scenario where you allowed your employee to use a company car knowing he was intoxicated and he subsequently caused a fatal accident.

In this situation, you could be held personally liable and your personal assets could be seized to compensate for the damages.

CHAPTER 11: UNRAVELING AN LLC

Initiating the dissolution of a company is a multi-step process that commences with the crucial decision to discontinue operations. Subsequent steps involve liaising with appropriate government bodies, filing final tax returns, and notifying creditors about your decision.

Call for a Dissolution Vote
A company's voluntary dissolution is a conscious choice made by its members.

This requires the consensus of all shareholders or adherence to predetermined circumstances which automatically trigger a dissolution, such as the demise of a business partner.

For the appropriate procedure, you should refer to your LLC operating agreement. In the event the agreement doesn't specify a dissolution clause, follow the procedures outlined in your state's LLC legislation. Once the decision has been finalized by a majority vote (or a dissolution-triggering event occurs), document this decision and store it with the company's official records.

Finalize Tax Returns
Before you can proceed with the dissolution, some states may necessitate clearance from the IRS or a certificate of good standing from your local tax agency. This is accomplished by submitting final tax returns and settling any remaining taxes. When filing, it's crucial to specify that it is the company's final return.

The tax authority will then issue a release in the form of a letter or certificate confirming that you are free from future tax liabilities. Regardless of whether your state mandates such clearance, it is essential to file your final state and federal tax returns. Submitting your final employment tax returns is also crucial to avoid personal liability for any outstanding payroll taxes.

File Dissolution Paperwork
A form known as the articles of dissolution is required to formally request the dissolution of your company. This can be obtained from the corporation division or secretary of state's website in your state. In some cases, the form may be referred to as a statement of dissolution or a certificate of termination.

The form usually requires details about the company and its members, including whether all liabilities have been settled and assets distributed. Most states require a filing fee, so ensure you include the correct amount. Once approved, you will receive a certificate of dissolution from the state—keep a copy for your records.

Address Outstanding Liabilities
Before you can file the articles of dissolution, some states mandate that you notify creditors. Creditors could include lenders, insurance companies, service providers, and suppliers. Some states

also require public notices in local newspapers.

In your notice, establish a deadline for creditors to make claims, noting that any claims made post-deadline will be dismissed. Your state's laws will dictate the exact deadline, but it typically ranges between 90 and 180 days. Notifying creditors is beneficial even if it isn't mandated, as it allows you to settle all obligations and reduces the chances of unforeseen liabilities surfacing in the future.

Distribute Remaining Assets

Once taxes and creditors have been settled, you can distribute any remaining assets, such as investments, profits, and physical goods, among the LLC's members. In the absence of an operating agreement, you will have to rely on state laws to guide the asset distribution process.

Execute Further Wind-Down Actions

To properly close your business, additional steps may be necessary.

These may include terminating your workforce and settling any severance agreements, paying final payroll taxes, canceling contracts and leases, revoking business licenses and permits, and notifying customers about your closing date.

Finally, you will need to close your business bank accounts, federal employer identification number (FEIN), and state tax identification number (if you have one).

CHAPTER 12: HARNESSING GOVERNMENT CONTRACTS

Securing Government Contracts: Crafting Your Proposal
Your business journey might have acquainted you with tasks like crafting bids or outlining project scopes for prospective clients.

However, these experiences might not entirely equip you for the peculiarities of drafting a federal contract proposal. Completing a Request for Quotation (RFQ) or a Request for Proposal (RFP) for an official entity can feel like navigating through extensive taxation paperwork or DMV forms.

Nonetheless, within the confines of these intricate sections and stringent agency guidelines, ample opportunities await to underscore your firm's uniqueness and value proposition.
Below, you will find the first three most common solicitation types, often encountered on SAM.gov or other portals listing government contract opportunities:
RFQ: Request for Quotations

A Request for Quotation constitutes the streamlined procurement procedure for governmental bodies, typically employed for contracts not exceeding $150,000. Despite being deemed simpler by federal standards, you might still find it more complex compared to project proposals your firm has generated for private sector clientele. To glean insights into effective RFQ crafting for a business in your sector, consider perusing previous RFQ submissions in the SAM.gov database.

RFP: Request for Proposals
Government entities resort to Requests for Proposals for larger, negotiable acquisitions, facilitating a dialogue between the governmental body and potential vendor about pricing and conditions before reaching a consensus.

The process is initiated by the government agency issuing an RFP, which details the contract's specifications, projected constraints, and the information that applicants must include within their proposal. If any RFP requirements bewilder you, seek clarification from the contracts manager before submitting your proposal; complete and precise information is crucial.

Invitation for Bid (IFB)
Government procurement procedures referred to as sealed solicitations or Invitations for Bid allow for no negotiation between the agency and the vendor.

The primary differentiator amongst qualified bidders is often the price point, with the submitted bid package regarded as final. Responding to an IFB requires utmost diligence in compiling your documents and determining your rates, given the non-negotiable and definitive nature of the procurement process.

If your bid exceeds the specified range or misses critical information, the agency is likely to reject your bid in favor of another contender, as no room exists for negotiations or revisions.

CHAPTER 13: NAVIGATING THE LABYRINTH OF LLCS

Unraveling the Complexities: Key Questions about LLCs

Are there any business sectors unable to form an LLC?

Yes, certain sectors and professionals are restricted from forming LLCs.

For example, those engaged in banking, insurance, and trust services often cannot establish LLCs. Additionally, some states (like California) prohibit certain licensed professionals, such as doctors, lawyers, accountants, and certain other licensed practitioners, from forming LLCs.

What is an LLC, exactly?

An LLC, or Limited Liability Company, is a unique business structure that combines elements from both corporations and partnerships. Similar to corporate shareholders, owners of an LLC enjoy "limited liability," meaning they aren't personally liable for business debts and claims. In contrast to corporations, the LLC is not taxed as a separate entity, with owners recording their share of business profits or losses on their personal tax returns.

What's the minimum number of people needed to form an LLC?

Legally, you can establish an LLC with just one member. For various reasons, LLCs are usually most suitable for businesses with no more than 35 owners or investors.

Can I transition my existing business into an LLC?

Absolutely. Partnerships and sole proprietorships can convert their business to an LLC to safeguard their personal assets, all while maintaining their existing tax structure. This book elaborates on how to utilize a "certificate of conversion" or standard articles of organization to transition to an LLC.

What steps must I take to form an LLC?

To legally establish an LLC in most states, you must file articles of organization with your state's LLC filing office, often a division of the Secretary of State's office. In some states, an additional step is needed: you must announce your intention to create an LLC in local media either before or immediately after filing your articles of organization.

How is an LLC taxed?

Interestingly, the LLC itself isn't taxed as a separate entity. Instead, LLC owners declare their share of the business profits (or record their share of losses) on their personal tax returns. It is also possible for LLC owners to choose to have their LLC taxed like a corporation, which can result in lower taxes for well-established members who often need to retain a significant portion of the business's profits.

Do I require a lawyer to form an LLC?

While not necessary, having a lawyer can be beneficial in certain situations. However, the process of forming an LLC is generally straightforward and can often be completed by downloading instructions and forms from your state's registration website.

Should I have an Operating Agreement for my LLC?

Although most state LLC statutes don't mandate a written operating agreement, it's unwise to operate an LLC without one. The agreement is vital as it sets rules for profit and loss allocation, governance of significant business decisions, and processes for member exits and additions. It also helps ensure courts will respect your personal liability protection by showcasing your due diligence in setting up your LLC.

How does an LLC differ from a partnership?

The key difference lies in liability: LLC owners aren't personally accountable for the company's debts and obligations, unlike partners. Furthermore, LLCs have to file official articles of organization, pay a filing fee, and comply with other state filing procedures before they can operate, which is not the case for partnerships.

Is an understanding of securities laws necessary to form an LLC?

For a single-member LLC that doesn't plan on accepting investments from third parties, understanding securities laws isn't critical. For co-owned LLCs, things get a bit more complex. In cases where some or all members are passive investors expecting to profit from others' work, their investment would usually be considered a security under state and federal law, requiring compliance with relevant securities regulations.

However, smaller LLCs, including those intending to sell shares to passive investors, often qualify for exemptions from securities laws.